اللباس الإسلامي للمرأة

ISLAMIC
DRESS CODE
FOR WOMEN

© **Maktaba Dar-us-Salam, 1999**

King Fahd National Library Catalog-in-Publication Data

Abdullah, Abdul Rahman

Islamic dress code for women-Riyadh

64p, 14x21 cm   **ISBN: 9960-899-44-6**

1-Women in Islam   II-Title

219.1dc   1425/2442

Legal Deposit no.1425/2442

ISBN: 9960-899-44-6

HEAD OFFICE

P.O. Box: 22743, Riyadh 11416 K.S.A.Tel: 0096 -1-4033962/4043432 Fax: 4021659
E-mail: riyadh@dar-us-salam.com, darussalam@awalnet.net.sa Website: www.dar-us-salam.com

K.S.A. Darussalam Showrooms:
  Riyadh
Olaya branch: Tel 00966-1-4614483 Fax: 4644945
Malaz branch: Tel 00966-1-4735220 Fax: 4735221
• **Jeddah**
  Tel: 00966-2-6879254 Fax: 6336270
• **Madinah**
  Tel: 00966-503417155 Fax: 04-8151121
• **Al-Khobar**
  Tel: 00966-3-8692900 Fax: 8691551
• **Khamis Mushayt**
  Tel & Fax: 00966-072207055
U.A.E
• **Darussalam, Sharjah U.A.E**
  Tel: 00971-6-5632623 Fax: 5632624
  Sharjah@dar-us-salam.com.
PAKISTAN
• **Darussalam,** 36 B Lower Mall, Lahore
  Tel: 0092-42-724 0024 Fax: 7354072
• **Rahman Market, Ghazni Street,**Urdu Bazar Lahore
  Tel: 0092-42-7120054 Fax: 7320703
• **Karachi,** Tel: 0092-21-4393936 Fax: 4393937
• **Islamabad,** Tel: 0092-51-2500237
U.S.A
• **Darussalam, Houston**
  P.O Box: 79194 Tx 77279
  Tel: 001-713-722 0419 Fax: 001-713-722 0431
  E-mail: houston @dar-us-salam.com
• **Darussalam, New York** 481 Atlantic Ave, Brooklyn
  New York-11217, Tel: 001-718-625 5925
  Fax: 718-625 1511
  E-mail: newyork@dar-us-salam.com.
U.K
• **Darussalam International Publications Ltd.**
  Leyton Business Centre
  Unit-17, Etloe Road, Leyton, London, E10 7BT
  Tel: 0044 20 8539 4885 Fax:0044 20 8539 4889
  Website: www.darussalam.com   ٭
  Email: info@darussalam.com
• **Darussalam International Publications Limited**
  Regents Park Mosque, 146 Park Road
  London NW8 7RG Tel: 0044- 207 725 2246
AUSTRALIA
• **Darussalam**، 153, Haldon St, Lakemba (Sydney)
  NSW 2195, Australia
  Tel: 0061-2-97407188 Fax: 0061-2-97407199
  Mobile: 0061-414580813 Res: 0061-2-97580190
  Email: abumuaaz@hotamail.com

CANADA
• Islmic Books Service
  2200 South Sheridan way Mississauga,
  Ontario Canada L5K 2C8
  Tel: 001-905-403-8406 Ext. 218 Fax: 905-8409
HONG KONG
• **Peacetech**
  A2, 4/F Tsim Sha Mansion
  83-87 Nathan Road Tsimbatsui
  Kowloon, Hong Kong
  Tel: 00852 2369 2722 Fax: 00852-23692944
  Mobile: 00852 97123624
MALAYSIA
• **Darussalam International Publication Ltd.**
  No.109A, Jalan SS 21/1A, Damansara Utama,
  47400, Petaling Jaya, Selangor, Darul Ehsan, Malaysia
  Tel: 00603 7710 9750 Fax: 7710 0749
  E-mail: darussalm@streamyx.com
FRANCE
• **Editions & Librairie Essalam**
  135, Bd de Ménilmontant- 75011 Paris
  Tél: 0033-01- 43 38 19 56/ 44 83
  Fax: 0033-01-43 57 44 31 E-mail: essalam@essalam.com·
SINGAPORE
• Muslim Converts Association of Singapore
  32 Onan Road The Galaxy
  Singapore- 424484
  Tel: 0065-440 6924, 348 8344 Fax: 440 6724
SRI LANKA
• **Darul Kitab** 6, Nimal Road, Colombo-4
  Tel: 0094 115 358712 Fax: 115-358713
INDIA
• **Islamic Dimensions**
  56/58 Tandel Street (North)
  Dongri, Mumbai 4000 009,India
  Tel: 0091-22-3736875, Fax: 3730689
  E-mail:sales@irf.net
SOUTH AFRICA
• Islamic Da`wah Movement (IDM)
  48009 Qualbert 4078 Durban,South Africa
  Tel: 0027-31-304-6883 Fax: 0027-31-305-1292
  E-mail: idm@ion.co.za

اللباس الإسلامي للمرأة

ISLAMIC DRESS CODE FOR WOMEN

Compiled by
Darussalam Research Division

Edited by
Abdul Rahmân Abdullâh
Formerly
Raymond J. Manderola
Fordham University, USA

DARUSSALAM
GLOBAL LEADER IN ISLAMIC BOOKS
Riyadh • Jeddah • Al-Khobar • Sharjah
Lahore • London • Houston • New York

In the Name of Allâh
the Most Gracious, the Most Merciful

"O you who believe, protect yourselves and
your families from a fire whose fuel are
men and stones." (*At-Tahrîm*, 66:6)

Contents

Publishers Note

In our world of chaos and confusion concerning the unending problems of sexual abuses and perversion, most of mankind, who does not have the benefit of Islamic knowledge and guidance, has all but given up hope on how to come to terms with this intractable of all problems.

Men who are embarrassed to face their own weaknesses boldly view the most lewd displays of psychologically damaging visual presentations. Women desperate for fame and fortune allow themselves to be presented as bait for the crudest commercial benefits. That which is naturally abhorrent becomes common place with the exposure and constant bombardment of illicit graphic exhibitions. What is the way out of this dilemma? How can we reclaim our self-respect and the respect of our community?

We have to forego the thrill of uncovering that, which was meant to be covered and we have to forego the thrill of exposing that, which was meant to be hidden. If we don't, the disaster that accompanies these crimes will be upon us as a whole. We will pay, our children will pay and our children's children will pay. This is certain.

Thankfully, as Muslims we have the guidance on how to avoid these problems from the beginning if we follow the laws set out for us by Allâh Who knows His creation. Learning the history of those who came before us and who have come to disaster and seeing contemporary non-Muslim societies being devoured and destroyed due to lack of guidance and knowledge should make us rush to the solutions that Allâh has provided for us. Prevention is better than cure.

Darussalam presents *Islamic Dress Code for Women* as a solution to one of the most difficult problems of our time. There is no doubt that woman is an object of beauty. This beauty is a very powerful force; Allâh has prescribed how this beauty must be dealt with so that it becomes a force for good and not a source of destruction. Actions are judged by intention in Islam and as such the intention of men concerning the beauty of women must be constantly guarded. The lowering of the eyes by men is a physical act, but without the intention of doing so to protect one's piety and obeying Allâh, we have stumbled and failed. The struggle to be chaste is the duty of both male and female and we have to cooperate in this struggle by following the very clear guidelines that Allâh and His Messenger ﷺ have set for us.

Abdul Malik Mujhaid
General Manager

Islamic *Jilbâb* (overgarment)

Relevant Qur'ânic Verses and authentic Prophetic traditions lay great emphasis on the observance of the woman's dress code. It is only by observing the Islamic dress code that modesty can be maintained. Islam stipulates certain conditions and requirements of the Islamic *Jilbâb*,[1] or woman's outer garment, that the *Muslimah* must observe when going out in particular. When the *Muslimah* goes out, she must wear an outer garment to cover the clothes she is wearing as well as any other beauty enhancements. Woman's *Jilbâb* may be considered proper and Islamic as long as it meets the following requirements:

1. Large enough to cover the whole body.
2. Plain, not decorative.
3. Close in texture and opaque.
4. Unperfumed.
5. Should not resemble men's clothes.
6. Should not resemble the disbelievers' clothes.
7. Should not be conspicuous or ostentatious.

It should be borne in mind that some of the above conditions apply to men also. If they are not met, the dress becomes unlawful to wear.

1. Large enough to cover the whole body

The reference to this requirement is in the Words of :

﴿ وَقُل لِّلْمُؤْمِنَٰتِ يَغْضُضْنَ مِنْ أَبْصَٰرِهِنَّ وَيَحْفَظْنَ فُرُوجَهُنَّ وَلَا يُبْدِينَ زِينَتَهُنَّ إِلَّا مَا ظَهَرَ مِنْهَا وَلْيَضْرِبْنَ بِخُمُرِهِنَّ عَلَىٰ جُيُوبِهِنَّ وَلَا يُبْدِينَ

---

[1] *Jilbâb*, literally means, a thing that prevents, debars, conceals or hides, because it prevents seeing or beholding. But in relation to women in Islam, it signifies women's outer garment.

زِينَتَهُنَّ إِلَّا لِبُعُولَتِهِنَّ أَوْ ءَابَآئِهِنَّ أَوْ ءَابَآءِ بُعُولَتِهِنَّ أَوْ
أَبْنَآئِهِنَّ أَوْ أَبْنَآءِ بُعُولَتِهِنَّ أَوْ إِخْوَٰنِهِنَّ أَوْ بَنِىٓ إِخْوَٰنِهِنَّ أَوْ بَنِىٓ
أَخَوَٰتِهِنَّ أَوْ نِسَآئِهِنَّ أَوْ مَا مَلَكَتْ أَيْمَٰنُهُنَّ أَوِ ٱلتَّٰبِعِينَ غَيْرِ أُوْلِى ٱلْإِرْبَةِ
مِنَ ٱلرِّجَالِ أَوِ ٱلطِّفْلِ ٱلَّذِينَ لَمْ يَظْهَرُواْ عَلَىٰ عَوْرَٰتِ ٱلنِّسَآءِ وَلَا يَضْرِبْنَ
بِأَرْجُلِهِنَّ لِيُعْلَمَ مَا يُخْفِينَ مِن زِينَتِهِنَّ وَتُوبُوٓاْ إِلَى ٱللَّهِ جَمِيعًا أَيُّهَ
ٱلْمُؤْمِنُونَ لَعَلَّكُمْ تُفْلِحُونَ ﴾ [النور : ٣١]

"And tell the believing women to lower their gaze and guard their *Furûj* (private parts), and disclose not their adornments except only that which is apparent , and that they should draw their headcovers over their *Juyûb* (bosoms), and that they disclose not their adornment except to their husbands, their fathers, or the fathers of their husbands, or their sons, or the sons of their brothers, or the sons of their sisters, or their women, or what their right hands possess,[2] or such of male attendants who have no sexual desire, or young children who have not attained the knowledge of women's private parts. And that they should not stamp their feet lest what they hide of their ornaments be known. And turn you to all together, O believers, that you may be successful." (V. 24:31)

Khimâr (headcloth), or headcover

This is the cloth which covers all of the hair on the head, while the word, '*Juyûb*' (pl. of *Jaib*) means not only the bosom, as commonly thought, but it includes the neck too. Imam Al-Qurtubi, an eminent Qur'ân commentator, states:

"Women in those days used to cover their heads with the *Khimâr,* throwing its ends on their backs, behind their ears leaving the neck, and the upper part of the chest uncovered, just as Christian women used to do. ,

---

[2] The possession of the right hand are the bondsmen and bondswomen.

later on, enjoined the Muslim women to cover with the *Khimâr* the upper part of their chests and the necks as well."

Allâh's Words: "And they should not stamp their feet," indicate clearly that woman's feet must be covered by the outer garment too. Women, in those days, used to wear anklets, and they would attract attention by making them tinkle together when stamping their feet.

'Abdullâh, son of 'Umar bin Khattâb رضى الله عنهما reported that 's Messenger ﷺ said:

"On the Day of Resurrection, will not look at the man who trails along his garment with pride." Thereupon, Umm Salamah رضى الله عنها asked, "What should women do with their garments?" The Prophet ﷺ said: "They should lower their garments a hand span," (half their shins down). Umm Salamah رضى الله عنها further said, "Women's feet would still be uncovered." 's Messenger ﷺ replied: "Let them lower them a forearm's length, but not longer. " (*At-Tirmidhi*)

The above Verse (24:31) quoted from *Sûrat An-Nûr*, gives specific detailed information as to what a *Muslimah* (Muslim woman) must wear to cover her body in the presence of strangers and non-*Mahram* relatives; whether indoors or outdoors. The Verse lists also the people with whom a woman is permitted to be less inhibited. While the following Verse quoted from *Sûrat Al-Ahzâb* commands the *Muslimah* to wear the *Jilbâb* (overgarment), be it a coat or a cloak, and draw it around her body.

Allâh says:

﴿ يَٰٓأَيُّهَا ٱلنَّبِيُّ قُل لِّأَزْوَٰجِكَ وَبَنَاتِكَ وَنِسَآءِ ٱلْمُؤْمِنِينَ يُدْنِينَ عَلَيْهِنَّ مِن جَلَٰبِيبِهِنَّ ذَٰلِكَ أَدْنَىٰٓ أَن يُعْرَفْنَ فَلَا يُؤْذَيْنَ وَكَانَ ٱللَّهُ غَفُورًا رَّحِيمًا ﴾

[الأحزاب : ٥٩]

"O Prophet! Tell your wives and your daughters, and the

women of the believers to draw their cloaks (veils) all over their bodies, that is more proper that they may be distinguished[3] and not be molested. And Allâh is Most Forgiving, Most Merciful." (V. 33:59)

The first Verse, clearly makes it incumbent upon women to conceal their beauty and adornment from strangers except that which might show unintentionally; such as the ring and the lower hem of the dress, and the like.

Covering the face and the hands was the practice of the Prophet's wives and other pious women during the time of 's Messenger ﷺ. Asmâ' رضى الله عنها said:

"We used to cover our faces from men." *(Al-Hâkim)*

'Âishah رضى الله عنها said:

"May Allâh grant the women of the *Ansâr* (the original Muslims of Al-Madinah), His Mercy, when Allâh revealed His Words, 'And that they draw their headcovers over their *Juyûb*,' they tore a portion of their wrapping garments and used them as *Khimâr* (headcloth)." *(Sahih Al-Bukhâri)*

2. Plain, not decorative

The Words of :

"… and that they disclose not their adornment …" (V. 24:31) apply in general to the outer garment, that is, it should not be decorative, colorful, conspicuous or eye-catching. Allâh says:

﴿ وَقَرْنَ فِي بُيُوتِكُنَّ وَلَا تَبَرَّجْنَ تَبَرُّجَ ٱلْجَٰهِلِيَّةِ ٱلْأُولَىٰ ﴾ [الأحزاب : ٣٣]

"And stay in your homes, and commit not *Tabarruj* (self-display) like the *Tabarruj* of the *Jâhiliyyah.*" (V. 33:33)

---

[3] The Muslim women were commanded to cover themselves up that they might be recognized as free women, and be distinguished from the pagan women and the slave-women, and be safe from being harassed or molested

Tabarruj of a woman is displaying her beauty and ornaments to strangers or men distantly related to her, and wearing in public, make-up or whatever may excite men's lust.

The purpose of *Jilbâb* is to conceal the details of the woman's body and her finery which she employs to enhance her appearance, but when the *Jilbâb* is colorful and decorative, it becomes an ornament in itself and defeats its own purpose.

In his renowned book, *Al-Kabâ'ir* (the Grave Sins), Imam Dhahabi asserts:

> "Among other things for which a woman would be cursed, are disclosing the fineries which she wears under her outer garment, wearing perfume in her outings, wearing a colorful outer garment, or a short cloak. *Tabarruj* includes all these things. Allâh the Exalted hates *Tabarruj* and the women who practice it."

Tabarruj is so abhorrent that Allâh's Messenger ﷺ considered it equal to *Shirk* (polytheism), fornication, stealing, and other reprehensible acts. 'Abdullâh bin 'Amr رضى الله عنه said:

> "Umaimah, daughter of Ruqaiyyah came to Allâh's Messenger ﷺ to give him her pledge of allegiance for Islam. He said to her, 'I accept your pledge of allegiance on the conditions that you will not associate partners with , nor steal, nor commit adultery, nor kill your children, nor commit a scandalous charge that you yourself forge, nor wail the dead, nor commit *Tabarruj* like that of the old *Jâhiliyyah*." (*Ahmad*)

Fadâlah bin 'Ubaid رضى الله عنه reported that Allâh's Messenger ﷺ said:

> "There are three people about whose evil fate you should not feel sorry: a man who seceded from the assembly of the Muslim *Ummah*, disobeyed his *Imâm* (the ruler of the Muslim *Ummah*), and died in that state; a slave who ran

13

away after having providing her with provisions but she displayed her beauty in *Tabarruj* during his absence. So do not be concerned about them." (*Ahmad*)

3. Close in texture and opaque

The *Jilbâb* (overgarment) must conceal the clothes underneath. Such requirements apply to the garment a *Muslimah* should wear for *Salât* as well. Flimsy and see-through garments make woman more exciting to men. The Prophet ﷺ referred to such women who wear thin garments as clothed-naked women. He said:

"There will be, in the latter days of my *Ummah*, women who will be dressed and yet undressed. (They will be wearing) on their heads (things) resembling camels' humps. Curse them. They are accursed." (*At-Tabarâni*)

In another tradition, Allâh's Messenger ﷺ referred to these women, saying:

"They shall not be admitted to *Jannah,* nor shall they smell its fragrance; although the fragrance of *Jannah* can be smelt from such and such distance (meaning from extremely long distance)." (*Sahih Muslim*)

'Dressed yet undressed women' are also those who wear tight and or transparent clothes, or clothes that reveal more than conceal. The Prophet ﷺ said:

"*Hayâ*' and *Imân* are tied together, if one of them departs, the other departs with it." (*Al-Hâkim*)

4. Unperfumed

A woman must avoid wearing perfume in public. There are many Prophetic traditions that forbid women from wearing perfume outside their homes. Abu Musa Al-Ash'ari رضى الله عنه reported that the Prophet ﷺ said:

"Any woman who wears perfume and passes by people who would smell her perfume, is a fornicator." (*An-Nasa'I* and *Abu Dâwud*)

14

A woman passed by Abu Hurairah رضى الله عنه wearing strong perfume. He asked her: "O slave of the Powerful! Are you going to the mosque?" "Yes," the woman answered. He further asked her, "Did you wear perfume for this purpose?" The woman answered, "Yes." Thereupon, he said, "Go back home and have a wash. I heard Allâh's Messenger ﷺ saying, 'Any woman who goes to the mosque wearing perfume, Allâh does not accept her *Salât* unless she returns home and washes off the smell of her perfume.'"

If it is prohibited for a woman to wear perfume for going to the mosque, it is certainly much more so to wear perfume when going to public places. The sin of doing so would be much greater. Al-Haithami asserted:

"When a woman goes out wearing make-up and perfume, she commits a grave sin even if her husband permits her to do so." (*Az-Zawâjir*)

'Abdullâh bin 'Umar رضى الله عنه reported that Allâh's Messenger ﷺ said:

"Three people Allâh will debar them from *Jannah*: an alcoholic, a person who is not dutiful to his parents, and a *Daiyûth* who approves perverted behavior of his wife." (*Ahmad*)

The epithet '*Daiyûth*' literally signifies a man who knows and tolerates his wife's infidelity, or one who does not feel jealous when his wife goes out wearing perfume and make-up, exciting men's lust consciously or unconsciously.

5. Should not resemble men's clothes

Abu Hurairah Allâh رضى الله عنه reported that Allâh's Messenger ﷺ cursed the man who wears women's clothes, and the woman who wears men's clothes. (*Ahmad, Abu Dâwud* and *Ibn Mâjah*)

'Abdullâh bin 'Amr bin 'Âs رضى الله عنهما said:

"I heard Allâh's Messenger ﷺ saying: 'He is not one of us who imitates women, nor is she who imitates men.'" (*Ahmad*)

When a woman wears men's clothes such as pants or jeans, and other men's outfits, she incurs upon herself the curse of Allâh and the curse of His Messenger ﷺ. The curse will affect her husband or her male guardian if he allows her to wear such outfits, because it is his responsibility to make sure she observes the Islamic dress code. Allâh the Exalted says:

﴿ يَٰٓأَيُّهَا ٱلَّذِينَ ءَامَنُوا۟ قُوٓا۟ أَنفُسَكُمْ وَأَهْلِيكُمْ نَارًا وَقُودُهَا ٱلنَّاسُ وَٱلْحِجَارَةُ ﴾

[التحريم: ٦]

"O you who believe, protect yourselves and your families from a fire whose fuel are men and stones." (V. 66:6)

And the Prophet ﷺ said:

"Everyone of you is a guardian, and everyone of you is responsible for his subordinates. The man is a guardian of his family, and he is responsible." (*Al-Bukhâri* and *Muslim*)

Some may argue that there is no harm in wearing men's clothes by women living in the West because this is prototypical of the Western women. This argument is groundless because Allâh has decreed that Muhammad ﷺ is the last of the Prophets and Messengers to whom He revealed the Qur'ân, the last of His Books, and He has chosen Islam as the only *Deen* accepted by Him. Islam, praise be to Allâh, is not subjected to men's whims or opinions. Allâh knows that Muslims will be living in non-Islamic societies, yet He has decreed that men should look different from women, and vice versa.

6. Should not resemble the disbelievers' clothes

Allâh says:

﴿ ثُمَّ جَعَلْنَٰكَ عَلَىٰ شَرِيعَةٍ مِّنَ ٱلْأَمْرِ فَٱتَّبِعْهَا وَلَا تَتَّبِعْ أَهْوَآءَ ٱلَّذِينَ لَا يَعْلَمُونَ ﴾ [الجاثية: ١٨]

"Then We have made you follow a set of laws, so

adhere to it, and follow not the inclinations of those who do not know." (V. 45:18)

The clause, 'who do not know,' includes all those who oppose the *Deen* of Muhammad ﷺ while 'their inclinations,' signifies all the falsehood and whims the disbelievers hold as part of their religion. When Muslims follow the disbelievers' whims they, in fact, approve indirectly of their religion.

Allâh, the Exalted, says:

﴿ ۞ أَلَمۡ يَأۡنِ لِلَّذِينَ ءَامَنُوٓاْ أَن تَخۡشَعَ قُلُوبُهُمۡ لِذِكۡرِ ٱللَّهِ وَمَا نَزَلَ مِنَ ٱلۡحَقِّ وَلَا يَكُونُواْ كَٱلَّذِينَ أُوتُواْ ٱلۡكِتَٰبَ مِن قَبۡلُ فَطَالَ عَلَيۡهِمُ ٱلۡأَمَدُ فَقَسَتۡ قُلُوبُهُمۡۖ وَكَثِيرٌ مِّنۡهُمۡ فَٰسِقُونَ ﴾ [الحديد: ١٦]

"Is it not high time that the believers should humble their hearts to the remembrance of Allâh and the truth which He has revealed and that they should be unlike those to whom the Book was given before, and to whom the term seemed over protracted so that their hearts hardened, and many of them are impious." (V. 57:16)

Sheikh-ul-Islam Ibn Taimiyah رحمه الله commented on this Verse saying:

"The Divine statement: 'They should be unlike those to whom the Book was given,' embodies a complete prohibition against imitating the disbelievers in general, and in particular against imitating them in their hard-heartedness which is a product of sin." (*Iqtidâ' As-Sirât Al-Mustaqim*)

Commenting on this Verse too in his exegesis, Ibn Kathir said:

"Hence, Allâh has forbidden His believing slaves to imitate the deeds and expressions of the disbelievers."

Allâh's Messenger ﷺ was very particular about commanding his followers to differ from the disbelievers, not only in social life, but also in acts of worship. We must, therefore, heed to the

17

Words of Allâh, and be mindful of His prohibitions. If we adopt the disbelievers' way of life, we would also actually partake of the quality of their hearts.

7. Should not be conspicuous or ostentatious

'Abdullah bin 'Umar Allâh رضى الله عنـــهما reported that Allâh's Messenger ﷺ said:

> "Whosoever wears a dress for pretentious show in this world, Allâh will give him to wear a dress of humiliation on the Day of Resurrection, then it will be set on fire." (Abu Dâwud)

A conspicuous or ostentatious garment is that which a person wears to be distinguished from others either because the garment is expensive, or simply to show it off. A person may also wear rags just to show his or her renunciation of worldly things, or out of hypocrisy.

Ibn-ul-Athir said:

> "Ostentation applies also to colors, when a person wears clothes of eye-catching colors so that he or she stands out or becomes the center of attention."[4]

Some other prohibitions

There are other prohibitions regarding personal appearance of which the Muslim sisters should be aware. Wearing a hairpiece, or wig, plucking facial hair, filing teeth and tattooing are prohibited by Allâh's Messenger ﷺ. Asmâ' رضى الله عنها reported:

> A woman asked Allâh's Messenger ﷺ: "I have a daughter who has just married. She contracted measles and lost her hair as a result; can she wear a wig?" Allâh's Messenger ﷺ denied her request saying: "Allâh curses the one who makes wigs, and the one who wears

---

[4] Muhammad bin Ali Ash-Shaukâni, *Nail-ul-Autâr*, vol. 2, p.94

them." (*Sahih Muslim*)

'Alqamah reported that 'Abdullah bin 'Umar رضى الله عنهما said:

> "Allâh has cursed the tattooers and the tattooed, those
> who have their facial hair plucked and those who pluck
> facial hair of others, and those who have their teeth filed
> and those who file others' teeth, who alter the creation
> of Allâh." A woman from Banu Asad, who used to read
> the Qur'ân came to him and asked: "What is this
> tradition I heard you are reporting? I heard that you have
> cursed the tattooed and the tattooer, those who have
> their facial hair plucked, and those who pluck facial hair
> of others, and those who have their teeth filed and those
> who file the teeth of others, who alter the creation of
> Allâh." 'Abdullâh bin 'Umar رضى الله عنهما Allâh
> responded: "Why should I not curse those whom Allâh's
> Messenger ﷺ has cursed. Besides, it is mentioned in the
> Book of Allâh?" The woman said: "I have read the
> Qur'ân from cover to cover but I did not find what you
> are saying." "If you read it," 'Abdullah bin 'Umar رضى الله
> عنهما said, "you should have found it. Allâh, says:

﴿ وَمَآ ءَاتَىٰكُمُ ٱلرَّسُولُ فَخُذُوهُ وَمَا نَهَىٰكُمۡ عَنۡهُ فَٱنتَهُواْ ﴾ [الحشر: ٧]

> "And whatever the Messenger gives you, take it; and
> whatever he forbids you, abstain from it." (V. 59:7)

> The woman said: "I noticed that your wife has violated
> some of (the prohibitions you are reporting)." He said:
> "Come on in and see for yourself." The woman went
> inside his house, and came out again and said, "I have
> noticed nothing on your wife." He responded: "Had she
> violated these prohibitions, I would have divorced her."
> (*Sahih Muslim*)

It is the duty of every Muslim woman to fulfill the above
requirements of the *Jilbâb* (overgarment). It is also the duty of
every Muslim man to see that his wife, daughter, sister, or any of

his female dependents observe the Islamic dress code. It is only obeying Allâh and His Messenger ﷺ through which we may prosper, deserve His pleasure, and avoid His wrath.

May Allâh help us strengthen our *Imân*, and be more obedient to Him and to His Prophet ﷺ, and to guard ourselves against the torment of Hell-fire.

Hijâb (veiling)

Islam is the chosen religion of Allâh. It is a complete code of life for all times. Its distinguishing feature is that it combines the requisites of the world and the Hereafter. It has abrogated all other religions, systems and ideologies. Now Islam stands out as a true religion leading mankind to salvation. Allâh says:

﴿ إِنَّ ٱلدِّينَ عِندَ ٱللَّهِ ٱلْإِسْلَٰمُ ﴾ [آل عمران: ١٩]

"Truly, the religion with Allâh is Islam." (V. 3:19)

﴿ وَمَن يَبْتَغِ غَيْرَ ٱلْإِسْلَٰمِ دِينًا فَلَن يُقْبَلَ مِنْهُ وَهُوَ فِي ٱلْآخِرَةِ مِنَ ٱلْخَٰسِرِينَ ﴾ [آل عمران: ٨٥]

"And whoever seeks a religion other than Islam, it will never be accepted of him, and in the Hereafter he will be one of the losers." (V. 3:85)

﴿ ٱلْيَوْمَ أَكْمَلْتُ لَكُمْ دِينَكُمْ وَأَتْمَمْتُ عَلَيْكُمْ نِعْمَتِي وَرَضِيتُ لَكُمُ ٱلْإِسْلَٰمَ دِينًا ﴾ [المائدة: ٣]

"This day I have perfected your religion for you, completed My favor upon you; and have chosen for you Islam as your religion." (V. 5:3)

Islam teaches man how to differentiate between virtue and vice, enjoins him to do good and forbids him from evil so as to constitute a society based on truth, purity, justice and equality. Human nature is a blend of good and evil elements. That is why, sometimes man works righteousness and sometimes he acts sinfully. However, Allâh has opened the door of repentance and forgiveness. When a man turns to Allâh in repentance seeking forgiveness for his sins, Allâh forgives him. Of the sins some are major and others are minor. Minor sins are remitted with the practice of righteous deeds but the forgiveness of major sins requires the sinner to repent sincerely and determine not to repeat them in future. The major sins include polytheism, killing, disobedience to parents, usury and fornication as Allâh says:

﴿ ۞ قُلْ تَعَالَوْاْ أَتْلُ مَا حَرَّمَ رَبُّكُمْ عَلَيْكُمْ أَلَّا تُشْرِكُواْ بِهِۦ شَيْئًا وَبِٱلْوَٰلِدَيْنِ إِحْسَٰنًا وَلَا تَقْتُلُوٓاْ أَوْلَٰدَكُم مِّنْ إِمْلَٰقٍ نَّحْنُ نَرْزُقُكُمْ وَإِيَّاهُمْ وَلَا تَقْرَبُواْ ٱلْفَوَٰحِشَ مَا ظَهَرَ مِنْهَا وَمَا بَطَنَ وَلَا تَقْتُلُواْ ٱلنَّفْسَ ٱلَّتِى حَرَّمَ ٱللَّهُ إِلَّا بِٱلْحَقِّ ﴾ [الأنعام: ١٥١]

"Say (O Muhammad): Come I will recite whatever your Lord has prohibited you from: Join not anything in worship with Him; be good and dutiful to your parents; kill not your children because of poverty. We provide sustenance for you and for them; come not near to *Al-Fawâhish* (shameful sins and illegal sexual intercourse)." (V. 6:151)

Fornication is an unlawful contact between man and woman. It is prohibited by Allâh as He says:

﴿ وَلَا تَقْرَبُواْ ٱلزِّنَىٰٓ إِنَّهُۥ كَانَ فَٰحِشَةً وَسَآءَ سَبِيلًا ﴾ [الإسراء: ٣٢]

"And come not near to the unlawful sexual intercourse. Verily, it is a *Fâhishah* (i.e., anything that transgresses its limits), and an evil way (that leads one to Hell unless Allâh forgives him)." (V. 17:32)

Fornication is one of the sins that are rampant due to natural desire and sexual pleasure. In most of the cases, this contact remains secret between the two parties. Like killing or stealing, it does not have immediate aftereffects unless the woman conceives without marriage. As the religion of nature in the Words of Allâh:

﴿ فِطْرَتَ ٱللَّهِ ٱلَّتِى فَطَرَ ٱلنَّاسَ عَلَيْهَا لَا تَبْدِيلَ لِخَلْقِ ٱللَّهِ ذَٰلِكَ ٱلدِّينُ ٱلْقَيِّمُ ﴾ [الروم: ٣٠]

"Allâh's *Fitrah* (i.e., Allâh's Islamic Monotheism) with which He has created mankind. Let there be no change in

Khalqillâh (i.e., the religion of Allâh – Islamic Monotheism): that is the straight religion." (V. 30:30)

Islam does not curb natural desires but co-ordinates them properly so that man and woman cannot feel inclined to unlawful activities. To prevent mankind from falling into trial, the Islamic *Shari'ah* has devised three methods as given below:

1) Purification of the hearts:

In Islamic perspective, man is responsible before Allâh, the Lord of the worlds, Who will call him to account on the Day of Judgment. Then, Allâh will reward him for his deeds. The righteous will enjoy Divine Pleasure. All blessings will be at their disposal. While the transgressors will be doomed to punishment that cannot be imagined. The evidences from the Qur'ân and *Hadith* confirm that the punishment will be severe as Allâh says:

﴿ إِنَّ ٱلَّذِينَ يُحِبُّونَ أَن تَشِيعَ ٱلۡفَٰحِشَةُ فِي ٱلَّذِينَ ءَامَنُوا۟ لَهُمۡ عَذَابٌ أَلِيمٌ فِي ٱلدُّنۡيَا وَٱلۡأٓخِرَةِ ﴾ [النور : ١٩]

"Verily, those who like that (the crime of) illegal sexual intercourse should be propagated among those who believe, they will have a painful torment in this world and in the Hereafter." (V. 24:19)

2) Imposition of limits and punishments:

Allâh has gradually set the rules for punishment of adultery. First of all, He revealed the Verse:

﴿ وَٱلَّذَانِ يَأۡتِيَٰنِهَا مِنكُمۡ فَـَٔاذُوهُمَا فَإِن تَابَا وَأَصۡلَحَا فَأَعۡرِضُوا۟ عَنۡهُمَآ إِنَّ ٱللَّهَ كَانَ تَوَّابًا رَّحِيمًا ﴾ [النساء : ١٦]

"And the two persons (man and woman) among you who commit illegal sexual intercourse, hurt them both. And if they repent (promise Allâh that they will never repeat, i.e., commit illegal sexual intercourse and other similar sins) and do righteous good deeds, leave them alone. Surely, Allâh is Ever All-Forgiving (the One

23

Who forgives and accepts repentance), (and He is) Most Merciful." (V. 4:16)

Along with the punishment for the fornicator, Allâh ordained to detain the woman in the house. Then, Allâh determined the punishment for them:

﴿ ٱلزَّانِيَةُ وَٱلزَّانِي فَٱجْلِدُوا۟ كُلَّ وَٰحِدٍ مِّنْهُمَا مِا۟ئَةَ جَلْدَةٍ وَلَا تَأْخُذْكُم بِهِمَا رَأْفَةٌ فِى دِينِ ٱللَّهِ إِن كُنتُمْ تُؤْمِنُونَ بِٱللَّهِ وَٱلْيَوْمِ ٱلْءَاخِرِ وَلْيَشْهَدْ عَذَابَهُمَا طَآئِفَةٌ مِّنَ ٱلْمُؤْمِنِينَ ﴾

[النور : ٢]

"The fornicatress and the fornicator, flog each of them with a hundred stripes. Let not pity withhold you in their case, in a punishment prescribed by Allâh, if you believe in Allâh and the Last Day. And let a party of the believers witness their punishment. [This punishment is for unmarried persons guilty of the above crime (illegal sex) but if married persons commit it, the punishment is to stone them to death according to Allâh's Law]." (V. 24:2)

He also ordered to stone the adulterous man and woman to death. This order was executed by the Prophet ﷺ and his rightly-guided caliphs. In addition to the above, Allâh has called to boycott those involved in fornication as He says:

﴿ ٱلزَّانِى لَا يَنكِحُ إِلَّا زَانِيَةً أَوْ مُشْرِكَةً وَٱلزَّانِيَةُ لَا يَنكِحُهَآ إِلَّا زَانٍ أَوْ مُشْرِكٌ وَحُرِّمَ ذَٰلِكَ عَلَى ٱلْمُؤْمِنِينَ ﴾ [النور : ٣]

The adulterer–fornicator marries not but an adulteress-fornicatress or a female polytheist and the adulteress, none marries her except an adulterer–fornicator or a polytheist (and that means that the man who agrees to marry a female polytheist or a prostitute, then he is either an adulterer–fornicator, or a polytheist; and the woman who agrees to marry a polytheist or an adulterer –fornicator, then she is either a prostitute or a female polytheist). Such a thing is forbidden to the believers." (V. 24:3)

In order to purify the hearts, Allâh has decreed to produce four witnesses against those involved in adultery. In case of a false allegation, He has ordered to punish the accuser as mentioned in the Qur'ân:

﴿ وَٱلَّذِينَ يَرْمُونَ ٱلْمُحْصَنَٰتِ ثُمَّ لَمْ يَأْتُوا۟ بِأَرْبَعَةِ شُهَدَآءَ فَٱجْلِدُوهُمْ ثَمَٰنِينَ جَلْدَةً وَلَا نَقْبَلُوا۟ لَهُمْ شَهَٰدَةً أَبَدًا ۚ وَأُو۟لَٰٓئِكَ هُمُ ٱلْفَٰسِقُونَ ٠ إِلَّا ٱلَّذِينَ تَابُوا۟ مِنۢ بَعْدِ ذَٰلِكَ وَأَصْلَحُوا۟ فَإِنَّ ٱللَّهَ غَفُورٌ رَّحِيمٌ ﴾ [النور : ٤-٥]

"And those who accuse chaste women, and produce not four witnesses, flog them with eighty stripes, and reject their testimony forever. They indeed are the transgressors. Except those who repent thereafter and do righteous deeds; (for such) verily, Allâh is Oft-Forgiving, Most Merciful." (V. 24:4, 5)

In this way, Allâh has prohibited people to tarnish the character of the pious persons.

3) Marriage:

To keep man away from unlawful sexual contact, Allâh has decreed marriage and has allowed the bridal-money to be very small such as an iron-ring, shoes, porridge made of wheat or barley and the memorization of some Verses or Chapters of the Qur'ân. Man can marry two, three and four women according to his physical ability and financial resources. To deal with cases of irreconcilable differences, Allâh has given him the right of divorce in unavoidable circumstances, though it is an abominable act before Allâh. The reason it is so discouraged is that the conjugal relation is meant for the whole life in the interest of the children and the society. Anyhow, Allâh has also given woman the right of abolishing the marriage contract through *Khul'* (divorce at the instance of wife against payment of certain amount of money) as well as the option to cancel the marriage, concluded in young age, after reaching the age of puberty. By such means, man and woman can lead a happy life

25

fulfilling their sexual desire lawfully and safely. But it is pity that even after marriage, some people are inclined to make illegal contact with other women. Unfortunately, we have become so weak that we feel any temptation put in front of us is an excuse to fail our test and give in to our desires. Man walks around hoping the woman makes a mistake so he can have an excuse to make a mistake. Men are to be blamed firstly because they are responsible for the governance of their subjects. So if one man doesn't teach those females under his responsibility how to act like a *Muslimah*, some other man will be tempted by her. If a pretty woman shows her beauty publicly, anyone would feel inclined to, at least, look at her and admire her beauty which are the first steps in the wrong direction. In view of the human phenomenon, that man is weak to the allure of a woman and a woman can find it hard to resist using this power of hers, Allâh has ordered that women should draw cloaks over their body. He has also prevented woman from stamping their feet lest their anklets and other ornaments should tinkle to attract men towards them. Allâh's Messenger has also hindered woman from wearing make-up and perfume while going outside. He says:

«كُلُّ عَيْنٍ زَانِيَةٌ ،وَالْمَرْأَةُ إِذَا اسْتَعْطَرَتْ فَمَرَّتْ بِالْمَجْلِسِ فَهِيَ كَذَا»

"Every eye is adulterous and when a woman passes by a company (of men), she is such and such (meaning adulterous)." (*At-Tirmidhi* and *Abu Dâwud*)

It is a fact that a woman's motions, eyes, laughing, adornment and see-through clothes excite the lusts and stir up the emotions. They can be controlled only by adhering to the orders and prohibitions from Allâh. Therefore, it is imperative for a Muslim woman to wear a veil to hide her charm, clothing and ornaments; and to refrain from being a source of temptation. Satan is a manifest enemy of man. He attacks at the weak points of human nature and tries all tactics to trap man and woman in sin. In this context, every Muslim should understand the rationale of veiling and observe the rules relevant to it so that one may avoid the displeasure of Allâh and His Messenger ﷺ. On this occasion, it is worthy to note that the face of a woman is the most important part of her beauty. The face is the manifestation of a woman's beauty. Seeing its features and complexion, man begins to love a woman. It is the root cause of sexual excitement. Poets and prose-writers have highly appreciated it using excellent similitudes and metaphors to describe it. In short, a woman's face is the part that attracts the hearts, excites the passions and stirs up the lusts. Therefore, it is necessary to hide it most. Next are the hands and feet. Normally, they are open out of the dress but from Islamic point of view they should also be covered.

In regard to veiling, there are three different schools of thought: Some religious scholars claim that the order of *Hijâb* does not include the face and palms. The Muslims have obligated it upon themselves at their own accord, as there is no evidence in the Qur'ân and *Hadith* to hide the face and palms. But in fact, these scholars have stumbled in their interpretation of the *Hijâb* rulings, which are very clear. Some scholars emphasize *Satr* (covering of certain parts of body). They assert that the *Hijâb* is related to certain parts of the body that should be covered. Accordingly, a group of them consider the face and the palms as the parts to be covered. In support of their view, they bring forth the following Verse:

﴿ وَإِذَا سَأَلْتُمُوهُنَّ مَتَٰعًا فَسْـَٔلُوهُنَّ مِن وَرَآءِ حِجَابٍ ﴾ [الأحزاب : ٥٣]

"And when you ask them for anything you want, ask them from behind a screen." (V. 33:53)

'Ask them from behind the screen' means that no one should see the woman's face or her palms or her feet. In this way, it is right to say that the face together with the palms and feet are to be covered. While another group strongly opposes the supporters of the above view and declares that the face and palms are excluded from the parts to be covered; but they have no sound proof in favor of their stance.

27

The majority of religious scholars are of the opinion that veiling applies to all parts of body including face, palms and feet in the light of the evidence from the Qur'ân and *Hadith*.

The Muslim *Ummah* has committed to it all through the ages in obedience to the orders of Allâh and His Messenger ﷺ.

From the above, it is evident that veiling is unavoidable for woman. Allâh and His Messenger ﷺ have ordered woman to draw cloaks before strangers and distant relatives. Therefore, she must observe it. The veil is especially meant for the head, face, hair, hands, bosom, feet and other parts of the body. To hide them, the *Jilbâb* is the best thing. The *Jilbâb* is a long, plain and flowing garment that covers the entire body. On the other hand, Allâh has ordered men to lower their gaze and safeguard their private parts as mentioned in the Qur'ân:

﴿ قُل لِّلْمُؤْمِنِينَ يَغُضُّوا۟ مِنْ أَبْصَٰرِهِمْ وَيَحْفَظُوا۟ فُرُوجَهُمْ ﴾ [النور : ٣٠]

"Tell the believing men to lower their gaze and protect their private parts (from committing illegal sexual acts)." (V. 24:30)

Therefore, it is not allowed to undermine the veiling or deride it as a means of humiliation for women. Islam deals with no one unjustly. Rather, it has observed the rights of all. As a human being, men and women are equal before Allâh. However, due to their physical structure, Allâh has assigned them different jobs so as to maintain a check and balance in the society. Man is the supporter of the family while woman is responsible for the household. Man earns money while woman spends it, manages the house, brings up the children, provides them basic education and cares for the husband. If a woman gets a happy and honored life in the house, there is nothing wrong with it. Islam is not so strict to prevent woman from going outside and earning money at a time of need. If a woman's husband dies and she has no means of support, she can work outside for her livelihood while observing the rules of veiling. In the time of the Prophet ﷺ,

women used to take part in *Jihâd*, give water to the injured and bandage them. Some of them even used to work for their livelihood. For example, the wife of the well-known Companion, Abdullâh bin Mas'ud رضى الله عنــه, used to do handiwork and pay *Zakât* to her poor husband who had no job. The Prophet ﷺ approved of this act. So, it is not blameworthy for a woman to go outside to earn her sustenance when needed. Islam has laid down certain rules that the women should abide by.

The definition of veil

Veil is legitimately defined as the dress that covers the whole body of the woman including her head, face, hands and feet. It should be long, loose and plain not defining her shape. Veil has been prescribed for women to block the road to sin. In short, veiling is a source of covering the face, hands, feet and other parts of the body. Allâh says:

﴿ وَلْيَضْرِبْنَ بِخُمُرِهِنَّ عَلَىٰ جُيُوبِهِنَّ ﴾ [النور: ٣١]

"And they should draw their veils over their bosoms." (24:31)

﴿ يَـٰٓأَيُّهَا ٱلنَّبِىُّ قُل لِّأَزْوَٰجِكَ وَبَنَاتِكَ وَنِسَآءِ ٱلْمُؤْمِنِينَ يُدْنِينَ عَلَيْهِنَّ مِن جَلَـٰبِيبِهِنَّ ذَٰلِكَ أَدْنَىٰٓ أَن يُعْرَفْنَ فَلَا يُؤْذَيْنَ ﴾ [الأحزاب: ٥٩]

"O Prophet! Tell your wives and your daughters and the women of the believers to draw their cloaks (veils) all over their bodies (except eyes to see the way). That will be better, that they should be known (as free respectable women) so as not to be annoyed." (V. 33:59)

The purpose of veiling:

The purpose of veiling is to safeguard woman from the biased looks of men and provide her a pure atmosphere at home so that she can perform her household duties properly and contribute to improve the whole society as Allâh says:

﴿ وَقَرْنَ فِى بُيُوتِكُنَّ وَلَا تَبَرَّجْنَ تَبَرُّجَ ٱلْجَـٰهِلِيَّةِ ٱلْأُولَىٰ ﴾ [الأحزاب: ٣٣]

"And stay in your houses, and do not display yourselves like that of the former times of ignorance." (V. 33:33)

History shows that the children, who were brought up by their mothers in observance of the social values and religious obligations, later became the leaders of the nation. They admitted that the credit of their booming career goes to their mothers who bestowed on them the qualities of sincerity, faithfulness, honesty, self-reliance and social service; and encouraged them to continue their education. Veiling gives an esteemed position to woman and protects her from sexual harassment by people. On the other hand, a woman, who displays her beauty and wears tight, short and transparent clothes, attracts men towards her. Consequently, they try to exploit her sexually using all possible techniques. Sometimes, woman also becomes weak and surrenders herself to the lust of men. Veiling provides security to woman and promotes a pure atmosphere in the society. But those who consider themselves as modern people, consider it a disgrace and construe it as shackles for the woman. In comparison to the right and wrong, this world and the Hereafter, Paradise and Hell, the observance of veiling is much smaller matter.

The rationale of veiling:

Woman is Allâh's beautiful creation. On one hand, she satisfies man's sexual desires and on the other hand, she plays a significant role in the growth of the human generations. No doubt, woman has a great attraction for a man. Due to this attraction, it is feared he will indulge in sins. Therefore, Allâh has forbidden man strictly from fornication and adultery. He has also forbidden woman from exhibiting her charm. Regarding make-up and perfume, it is permissible for woman to wear them in front of her husband and closely related members of the family as Allâh says:

﴿ وَلَا يُبْدِينَ زِينَتَهُنَّ إِلَّا لِبُعُولَتِهِنَّ أَوْ ءَابَآئِهِنَّ أَوْ ءَابَآءِ بُعُولَتِهِنَّ أَوْ أَبْنَآئِهِنَّ أَوْ أَبْنَآءِ بُعُولَتِهِنَّ أَوْ إِخْوَٰنِهِنَّ أَوْ بَنِىٓ إِخْوَٰنِهِنَّ أَوْ بَنِىٓ أَخَوَٰتِهِنَّ أَوْ نِسَآئِهِنَّ ﴾ [النور : ٣١]

"They will not reveal their adornment except to their husbands or their fathers, or their husband's fathers, or their sons, or their husband's sons, or their brothers or their brother's sons, or their sister's sons, or their (Muslim) women." (V. 24:31)

The conditions of veiling

For proper veiling it is not enough to wear a scarf, face veil, headcover or an outer garment. There are certain conditions to be met. They are as follows:

1. The outer garment should be long, loose and opaque.

2. It should hide the entire body of the woman starting from her head, hair, face, hands and bosom down to the toe of her feet.

3. Her anklets and bracelets should not tinkle to allure men towards her.

4. It must be plane and close in texture not to draw attention to the woman. Also, it should not be decorated with ostentatious colors and designs.

5. It must not be transparent that reveals the woman's shape or her inner clothes.

6. It should not be designed to resemble the clothing of the disbelieving women.

7. It should not be similar to men's outfits in colors or design as the Prophet ﷺ is reported as having said:

«لَعَنَ اللهُ الْمُتَشَبِّهِينَ مِنَ الرِّجَالِ بِالنِّسَاءِ وَالْمُتَشَبِّهَاتِ مِنَ النِّسَاءِ بِالرِّجَالِ».

"Allâh condemns those men who behave or act in a womanlike manner, and those women who behave or act in manlike manner."

8. It should not be perfumed at all as it is not permissible for the Muslim woman to wear perfume while leaving home for an outing. The Prophet ﷺ has said:

«كُلُّ عَيْنٍ زَانِيَةٌ، وَالْمَرْأَةُ إِذَا اسْتَعْطَرَتْ فَمَرَّتْ بِالْمَجْلِسِ فَهِيَ كَذَا»

"Every eye is adulterous and when a woman perfumes

herself and passes by a company (of men), she is such and such (meaning adulterous)." (*At-Tirmidhi* and *Abu Dâwud*)

The first Verse regarding veil was revealed in Al-Madinah when 'Umar bin Khattab admonished the Prophet's wife, Sawdah bint Zam'ah, while going outside without veil. Allâh says:

﴿ يَٰٓأَيُّهَا ٱلنَّبِيُّ قُل لِّأَزۡوَٰجِكَ وَبَنَاتِكَ وَنِسَآءِ ٱلۡمُؤۡمِنِينَ يُدۡنِينَ عَلَيۡهِنَّ مِن جَلَٰبِيبِهِنَّ ذَٰلِكَ أَدۡنَىٰٓ أَن يُعۡرَفۡنَ ﴾ [الأحزاب: ٩٥]

"O Prophet! Tell your wives and your daughters and the women of the believers to draw their cloaks (veils) all over their bodies (except eyes to see the way). That will be better, that they should be known (as free respectable women) so as not to be annoyed." (V. 33:59)

Generally, the veiling covers the whole body including head, face, hair, bosom, hands and feet. But in the absence of men it is permissible for woman to uncover her face as narrated by 'Âishah رضى الله عنها:

كَانَ الرُّكۡبَانُ يَمُرُّونَ بِنَا وَنَحۡنُ مَعَ رَسُولِ اللهِ ﷺ مُحۡرِمَاتٌ، فَإِذَا حَاذَوا بِنَا سَدَلَتۡ إِحۡدَانَا جِلۡبَابَهَا مِنۡ رَأۡسِهَا عَلَى وَجۡهِهَا فَإِذَا جَاوَزُونَا كَشَفۡنَاهُ. [أبو داود]

"Some riders passed by us while we were with Allâh's Messenger ﷺ in the state of ritual consecration. When they came face to face, one of us let down her cloak (veil) from her head on her face and when they preceded us, we uncovered it." (*Abu Dâwud*)

The advantages of veiling:

The veiling system contains a number of advantages particularly in a society where the rape, sexual molestation and disrespect of woman are very common. Some of them are listed below:

1. Veiling is a protection for Muslim woman against the behavior of the wicked.

2. It is an identity of the Muslim woman that distinguishes her

3. It gives her an honored position in the society.

4. It acts as a barrier between men and women to keep them away from sins.

5. It is a means for observing chastity of woman.

6. It awakens the fear of Allâh in the heart of man and woman and saves them from falling in the abyss of evil.

7. It teaches man to respect the veiled woman, provide her protection from the curious persons and ensure the uplift of the high morals and social values in the society.

The disadvantages of unveiling:

Due to mixing up with the non-Muslims particularly in the countries where the Muslims are in minority, the practice of unveiling has become a regular feature. But it is very harmful for the Muslim society. Unveiling has a number of disadvantages. Out of them some are as follows:

1. It is a violation of the Qur'ân and *Hadith*.

2. It shows woman's weakness in belief.

3. It is a cause of temptation for men and women.

4. It strips off her modesty that is an integral part of Faith as the Prophet ﷺ said:

$$«الْحَيَاءُ مِنَ الإِيمَانِ» .$$

"Modesty is a part of Faith." (*Al-Bukhâri*)

5. It subjects her to sexual harassment.

6. It hurts her dignity and feelings and it stains her chastity.

7. It prompts woman to take part in commercial Allâh advertisements and films as a showpiece and a source of enjoyment for the viewers.

Recommendations:

Here are some recommendations that must be adhered to by a

veiled woman when going out. They are as follows:

Veiling is the tradition of Muslim women. Since its prescription, the Prophet's wives, daughters and other believing Muslim women have strictly observed it. Today also, the Muslim ladies must keep it up. The veiled woman must understand the rationale of veiling and fulfill its requirements.

She must avoid wearing perfume and showing her finery in any way.

She must not be encouraging while dealing with men at the time of need.

She must be harsh in voice and avoid speaking softly, because it can be misconstrued as an invitation, to strangers.

She must not stamp her feet letting her anklets tinkle or any other action that calls attention towards herself.

She must be careful and reserved in her motions and even in looks while walking outside.

The women who display their beauty are often subjected to sexual exploitation by immoral people.

It is a fact that the life of the world is nothing but superficiality while the actual life is the life of the Hereafter where everyone will be rewarded for their deeds. The righteous will enjoy Allâh's Pleasure. All blessings will be at their disposal. While the sinners and transgressors will be doomed to punishment that cannot be imagined. The evidence from the Qur'ân and *Hadith* confirm that Allâh's punishment will be severe.

Therefore, it is incumbent upon them to be chaste and veiling is a must for woman. However, she can uncover her face in the presence of the people who are closely related to her. She can freely move in front of the men in her common dress that has prescribed in the pleasure and comfort of her home.

It is the face from which the brands of beauty gush forth,

passions are stirred up and the lusts are excited. The woman is bound to veil her hair, face, bosom, palms and feet according to the teachings of Islam.

As a matter of fact, the charm of woman is incorporated in her personality and dress. So, Allâh has ordered woman to draw cloaks and hide her beauty from the strangers and distant relatives.

Some Important Questions and Answers Concerning Islamic Dress Code

(The *Shari'ah* Rulings presented in this chapter are given by the Grand Mufti of Saudi Arabia Sheikh Ibn Baz, Sheikh Ibn Jibreen, Sheikh Ibn Uthaimin and others)

The Islamic *Hijâb*

Q. What is the Islamic *Hijâb*?

A. The Islamic *Hijâb* is for the women to cover everything that is forbidden for her to expose. That is, she covers everything that she must cover. The first of those bodily parts that she must cover is her face. It is the source of temptation and the source of people desiring her. Therefore, the woman must cover her face in front of those men that are not *Mahram* (those that she is forbidden to marry). As for those who claim that the Islamic *Hijâb* is to cover the head, shoulders, back, feet, shin and forearms while allowing her to uncover her face and hands, this is a very amazing claim. This is because it is well known that the source of temptation and looking is the face. How can one say that the *Sharî'ah* does not allow the exposure of the foot of the woman while it allows her to uncover her face? It is not possible that there could be in the esteemed, wise and noble *Sharî'ah* a contradiction. Yet everyone knows that the temptation from uncovering the face is much greater than the temptation that results from the uncovering of the feet. Everyone also knows that the most sought after aspect of the woman for men is the face. If you told a prospective groom that a woman's face is ugly but her feet are beautiful, he would not propose to such a woman. However, if you told him that her face was beautiful but her hands, palms, or shins were less than beautiful, he would still propose to her. From this, one can conclude that the face is the first thing that must be covered. There are also evidences from the Book of Allâh and the *Sunnah* of our Prophet 繠. There are also statements from the Companions, the leading Imams and the great scholars of Islam that indicate that it is obligatory for the woman to cover all of her body in the presence of non-*Mahram* men. This obviously indicates that it is obligatory upon the woman to cover her face in front of such men. However, this

38

is not the place to quote all those authorities. And Allâh knows best.

Verily, Allâh is Beautiful and He loves beauty

Q. My dear friend is a very good person, applying her religion and loving to do what is good. However, she has one thing about her: She always loves to be distinguished from her friends. For example, in her dress, she likes to be different from the others, while being properly covered, of course. She does not want anyone to be like her. It is so bad that if she finds out that one of her friends has bought the same outfit she has, she will never wear it again. The same is true for how she dresses her children and with respect to their furniture. She cannot stand to see anyone else having the same thing she has. However, at the same time, she is not envious against anyone nor does she wish that others would not have such bounties, even if it is more beautiful than what she possesses. The only thing she cares about is to be different from the others. Is this envy or arrogance, as we dislike this characteristic of her very much?

A. I do not know what is in the heart of that lady that makes her behave in that way. If it is envy, it is forbidden. But envy implies wishing that others would lose the bounty they possess and even working to destroy it. She does not do that. If it is arrogance and having an aversion for others sharing with her, then it is also forbidden. But the arrogance that is blameworthy is to reject the truth and look down upon people, that is, belittle them. It does not include liking good clothes for oneself. Verily, Allâh is beautiful and He loves beauty. Perhaps she simply likes to be different from others and have notoriety in her appearance. So one must look to see what is the cause for that. This might just be part of her character that sets in the hearts of some people without there being a forbidden cause behind it. Allâh knows best.

Sheikh Ibn Jibreen

Uncovering a woman in front of her husband's relatives

Q. Is it legally permissible for a woman to uncover in front of her husband's brothers and cousins? Is it allowed for a boy to sleep in the same bed with his mother or sister after he has reached the age of puberty?

A. First, the brothers and cousins of the husband are not *Mahram* for his wife simply because they are his brothers or cousins. Therefore, it is not allowed for his wife to uncover in front of them what she cannot uncover in front of non-*Mahram* men. This is true even if they are very pious and trustworthy. Allâh has delineated whom a woman may expose her beauty to in the Verse:

﴿ وَقُل لِّلْمُؤْمِنَٰتِ يَغْضُضْنَ مِنْ أَبْصَٰرِهِنَّ وَيَحْفَظْنَ فُرُوجَهُنَّ وَلَا يُبْدِينَ زِينَتَهُنَّ إِلَّا مَا ظَهَرَ مِنْهَا وَلْيَضْرِبْنَ بِخُمُرِهِنَّ عَلَىٰ جُيُوبِهِنَّ وَلَا يُبْدِينَ زِينَتَهُنَّ إِلَّا لِبُعُولَتِهِنَّ أَوْ ءَابَآئِهِنَّ أَوْ ءَابَآءِ بُعُولَتِهِنَّ أَوْ أَبْنَآئِهِنَّ أَوْ أَبْنَآءِ بُعُولَتِهِنَّ أَوْ إِخْوَٰنِهِنَّ أَوْ بَنِىٓ إِخْوَٰنِهِنَّ أَوْ بَنِىٓ أَخَوَٰتِهِنَّ أَوْ نِسَآئِهِنَّ أَوْ مَا مَلَكَتْ أَيْمَٰنُهُنَّ أَوِ التَّٰبِعِينَ غَيْرِ أُوْلِى ٱلْإِرْبَةِ مِنَ ٱلرِّجَالِ أَوِ ٱلطِّفْلِ ٱلَّذِينَ لَمْ يَظْهَرُواْ عَلَىٰ عَوْرَٰتِ ٱلنِّسَآءِ ﴾

[النور: ٣١]

"(Tell the believing women) not to reveal their adornments except to their husbands, their fathers, their husband's fathers, their sons, their husband's sons, their brothers or their brother's sons, or their sister's sons, or their (Muslim) women or the (female) slaves, or old male servants who lack vigor, or small children who have no sense of the shame of sex." (V. 24:31)

Therefore, neither the brothers of the husband nor the children of the brothers of the husband nor the husband's cousins are from that group, even though they are related to him. Allâh makes no distinction in this matter between pious people and others. This is safer for the honor of people. It also blocks the road to sin and evil. It is confirmed in an authentic *Hadith* that the Prophet ﷺ was asked about the male in-laws[5] and he said:

«الْحَمْوُ الْمَوْتُ».

"The in-laws are death." (*Al-Bukhâri* and *Muslim*)

from temptation. It also closes the door to evil. The Prophet ﷺ ordered that the children be separated in their bedding when they reach the age of ten. He said:

"Order your children to pray when they are seven years old. And spank them (to exhort them) to do it by the age of ten and separate them in their bedding." (*Abu Dâwud* and *Ahmad*)

Those who are not approaching the age of puberty, still must ask permission to enter upon their parents at three times during the day. These are the times in which one is more likely to be taking off his clothing and exposing the parts that are usually covered. This has been stressed by them being called times of privacy. Allâh says in the Qur'ân:

﴿ يَـٰٓأَيُّهَا ٱلَّذِينَ ءَامَنُوا۟ لِيَسْتَـٔذِنكُمُ ٱلَّذِينَ مَلَكَتْ أَيْمَـٰنُكُمْ وَٱلَّذِينَ لَمْ يَبْلُغُوا۟ ٱلْحُلُمَ مِنكُمْ ثَلَـٰثَ مَرَّٰتٍ مِّن قَبْلِ صَلَوٰةِ ٱلْفَجْرِ وَحِينَ تَضَعُونَ ثِيَابَكُم مِّنَ ٱلظَّهِيرَةِ وَمِنۢ بَعْدِ صَلَوٰةِ ٱلْعِشَآءِ ثَلَـٰثُ عَوْرَٰتٍ لَّكُمْ لَيْسَ عَلَيْكُمْ وَلَا عَلَيْهِمْ جُنَاحٌ بَعْدَهُنَّ طَوَّٰفُونَ عَلَيْكُم بَعْضُكُمْ عَلَىٰ بَعْضٍ كَذَٰلِكَ يُبَيِّنُ ٱللَّهُ لَكُمُ ٱلْـَٔايَـٰتِ وَٱللَّهُ عَلِيمٌ حَكِيمٌ ﴾ [النور: ٥٨]

---

[5] Other than the husband's father or sons.

"O you who believe! Let your slaves and those among you who have not come to the age of puberty, ask permission (before they come to your presence) on three occasions: before morning prayer, and while you put off your clothes for the noonday (rest) and after the '*Isha* ' (Night) prayer. (These) three times are times of privacy for you. Other than those times there is no sin for you or for them to move about, attending to each other. Thus makes clear His signs to you. And is All-Knowing, All-Wise." (V. 24:58)

However, those who are past the age of puberty, must seek permission to enter at all times of the day. Allâh says:

﴿ وَإِذَا بَلَغَ ٱلْأَطْفَٰلُ مِنكُمُ ٱلْحُلُمَ فَلْيَسْتَـْٔذِنُوا۟ كَمَا ٱسْتَـْٔذَنَ ٱلَّذِينَ مِن قَبْلِهِمْ كَذَٰلِكَ يُبَيِّنُ ٱللَّهُ لَكُمْ ءَايَٰتِهِۦ وَٱللَّهُ عَلِيمٌ حَكِيمٌ ﴾

[النور: ٥٩]

"And when the children among you reach the age of puberty, then let them (also) ask for permission, as those senior to them (in age ask permission). Thus Allâh makes clear His signs for you. And Allâh is All-Knowing, All-Wise." (V. 24:59)

All of this is to avoid any kind of problems and temptations and to safeguard honor. It also brings an end to the means that lead to evil.

As for the child who is less than ten years old, it is permissible for him to sleep with his mother and sister in their bedding if there is some need to look after him and if there is no fear of temptation. They may also all sleep in the same area, in their own bedding, if they are of the age of puberty if there is no fear of temptation.

The Standing Committee

Uncovering one's face in front
of the servant

Q. What is the ruling concerning dealing with servants and family chauffeurs? Are they considered non-*Mahram*? My mother wants me to uncover my face in front of the servant and just put a scarf over my head. Is this allowed in our pure religion that orders us not to disobey the commands of Allâh?

A. The chauffeur and servants are like any other men and one must wear *Hijâb* (veil) in front of them if they are not *Mahram*. It is also not permissible to travel (alone) with them or to be in private with them. This is because the Prophet ﷺ said:

«لَا يَخْلُونَّ رَجُلٌ بِامْرَأَةٍ فَإِنَّ الشَّيْطَانَ ثَالِثُهُمَا»

"A man is never alone with a woman except that Satan is the third." (*Ahmad* and *At-Tirmidhi*)

This is also the case due to the generality of the evidence concerning the obligation of *Hijâb* and the prohibition of exposing one's beauty and body to anyone other than *Mahram* men. It is not allowed to obey one's mother or anyone else in something that is disobedience to Allâh.

Sheikh Ibn Baz

Uncovering one's face while abroad

Q. When we travel outside of Saudi Arabia, is it allowed for me to uncover my face and take off the *Hijâb* (veil) because I am away from my land and no one there will know me? My mother becomes impossible and is encouraging my father to force me to uncover my face because they consider me to be always looked by them (people) when I cover my face.

A. It is not allowed for you or any other woman like you to uncover her face in the lands of the disbelievers, in the same way that it is not allowed for you to do so in the land of the Muslims. It is obligatory to wear *Hijâb* in front of non-related men regardless if they be Muslims or disbelievers. In fact, it is more important to cover in front of the disbelievers because they have no Faith that will keep them from doing what has forbidden. It is also not allowed for you or anyone similar to you to obey your parents or others in doing something that Allâh and His Messenger ﷺ have forbidden. In *Sûrat Al-Ahzâb*, Allâh has stated:

$$\text{﴿ وَإِذَا سَأَلْتُمُوهُنَّ مَتَـٰعًا فَسْـَٔلُوهُنَّ مِن وَرَآءِ حِجَابٍ ذَٰلِكُمْ أَطْهَرُ لِقُلُوبِكُمْ وَقُلُوبِهِنَّ ﴾ [الأحزاب: ٥٣]}$$

"And when you ask them, ask them from behind a screen, that is purer for your hearts and for their hearts." (V. 33: 53)

Allâh shows in this noble Verse that women must wear *Hijâb* in front of non-*Mahram* men as that is purer for all of their hearts. In *Sûrat An-Nûr*, Allâh states:

$$\text{﴿ وَقُل لِّلْمُؤْمِنَـٰتِ يَغْضُضْنَ مِنْ أَبْصَـٰرِهِنَّ وَيَحْفَظْنَ فُرُوجَهُنَّ وَلَا يُبْدِينَ زِينَتَهُنَّ إِلَّا مَا ظَهَرَ مِنْهَا وَلْيَضْرِبْنَ بِخُمُرِهِنَّ عَلَىٰ جُيُوبِهِنَّ وَلَا يُبْدِينَ زِينَتَهُنَّ إِلَّا لِبُعُولَتِهِنَّ أَوْ ءَابَآئِهِنَّ أَوْ ءَابَآءِ بُعُولَتِهِنَّ أَوْ أَبْنَآئِهِنَّ أَوْ أَبْنَآءِ بُعُولَتِهِنَّ أَوْ إِخْوَٰنِهِنَّ أَوْ بَنِىٓ إِخْوَٰنِهِنَّ أَوْ بَنِىٓ أَخَوَٰتِهِنَّ أَوْ نِسَآئِهِنَّ أَوْ مَا مَلَكَتْ أَيْمَـٰنُهُنَّ أَوِ ٱلتَّـٰبِعِينَ غَيْرِ أُوْلِى ٱلْإِرْبَةِ مِنَ ٱلرِّجَالِ أَوِ ٱلطِّفْلِ ٱلَّذِينَ لَمْ يَظْهَرُوا۟ عَلَىٰ عَوْرَٰتِ ٱلنِّسَآءِ ﴾ [النور: ٣١]}$$

"Tell the believing women to lower their gaze and protect their private parts and not to show off their adornments except that which is apparent, and to draw their veils over necks and bosoms and not to reveal their adornments except to their husbands, their fathers, their husband's fathers, their sons, their husband's sons, their brothers or their brother's sons, or their sister's sons, or their (Muslim) women or the (female) slaves, or old male servants who lack vigor, or small children who have no sense of the shame of sex." (V. 24:31)

Obviously, the face is one of the greater sources of beauty a woman has.

Sheikh Ibn Baz

Short dresses for young children

Q. Some women, may Allâh guide them, dress their young daughters in short dresses that display the shins. When we advise those women, they answer, "We used to wear those when we were young and they did not cause us any harm when we got older." What is your opinion of that?

A. I am of the opinion that a person should not dress his daughter in such clothing while she is young. This is because if she grows accustomed to it, she will stick with it and she will consider it a light matter. However, if you trained her properly to be bashful when she was young, she would continue in that proper manner when she gets older. I advise my Muslim sisters to leave the dress of the foreigners who are the enemies of the religion and to bring up their children wearing clothes that cover their bodies, and to teach them modesty, for modesty is part of Faith.

Sheikh Ibn Uthaimin

The *Hijâb* of a young girl

Q. What is the ruling concerning young girls who have not reached the age of puberty? Is it allowed for them to go out without covering themselves? Can they pray without wearing a head covering?

A. It is a must that their guardians bring them up and teach them the manners of Islam. They should tell them not to go outside unless their bodies are covered. This is in order to avoid any temptation and to get them used to the virtuous manners so that they will not be a source of spreading evil. They should be ordered to pray with a head covering. If they pray without it, their prayers are not accepted. This is because the Prophet ﷺ said:

«لَا يَقْبَلَ اللهُ صَلَاةَ حَائِضٍ إِلَّا بِخِمَارٍ».

"Allâh does not accept the prayer of a female who has reached the age of puberty except if she is wearing a head covering (Khimâr)." (At-Tirmidhi, Ahmad, Abu Dâwud and Ibn Mâjah)

The Standing Committee

Hijâb of an elderly woman

Q. Is it allowed for a woman advanced in age, say 70 or 90 years old, to uncover her face in front of relatives who are not *Mahram*?

A. Allâh says:

﴿ وَٱلۡقَوَٰعِدُ مِنَ ٱلنِّسَآءِ ٱلَّٰتِي لَا يَرۡجُونَ نِكَاحًا فَلَيۡسَ عَلَيۡهِنَّ جُنَاحٌ أَن يَضَعۡنَ ثِيَابَهُنَّ غَيۡرَ مُتَبَرِّجَٰتٍۭ بِزِينَةٍۖ وَأَن يَسۡتَعۡفِفۡنَ خَيۡرٌ لَّهُنَّۗ وَٱللَّهُ سَمِيعٌ عَلِيمٌ ﴾ [النور : ٦٠]

"And as for women past child-bearing who do not expect marriage, it is no sin upon them if they discard their (outer) clothing in such a way as not to show their adornment. But to refrain is better for them. And Allâh is All-Hearer, All-Knower." (V. 24:60)

So there is no harm if the menopausal women who are not seeking marriage and are not displaying their adornments uncover their faces in front of non-related men. However, for them to remain covered is still better for Allâh has said in the Verse:

46

"But to refrain is better for them."

This is because some of them, when they are seen, may be a source of temptation due to their beautiful faces even though they are elderly and not displaying their adornments. However, if she is going to be having adornments (such as make-up and jewelry), she may not take off her outer covering. Having adornments includes beautifying the face with kohl and so forth.

Sheikh Ibn Baz

The *Hijâb* of a female servant

Q. Is it necessary for a female servant who works in the house to wear *Hijâb* in front of her employer?

A. Yes, she must wear *Hijâb* (veil) in front of him and she may not display her adornments in front of him. Also, it is forbidden for them to be in private due to general evidence prohibiting this. This is because if she does not wear *Hijâb* or she displays her adornments, she will be a source of temptation for him. Similarly, being in private is an opportunity for Satan to make them alluring and tempting.

Sheikh Ibn Baz

The female servant must wear *Hijâb*

Q. We have a Muslim female servant who performs all of her religious obligations except she does not cover her hair. Is it obligatory upon me to instruct her in this matter?

A. It is obligatory upon you to order her to cover her hair, face and the remainder of her body in order to be away from temptation and the spreading of evil.

The Standing Committee

Hijâb in front of non-Muslim women

Q. We have non-Muslim female servants in our house. Is it obligatory upon us to wear *Hijâb* in front of them? Is it allowed for me to give them my clothes to wash and then I pray in them? Is it allowed for me to explain the falsehood of their religion to them and to explain the distinguishing features of our pure religion?

A. First, it is not obligatory to wear *Hijâb* in front of them. They are like any other women according to the strongest of the two opinions among the scholars. There is no harm in them washing your clothing or utensils. However, it is obligatory to put an end to their contract because they have not embraced Islam. This is because in the Arabian Peninsula it is not allowed to have anyone except Muslims. Only Muslims may be hired in this Peninsula, regardless if it be workers, servants or whatever, regardless if they be men or women. This is because the Prophet ﷺ ordered that the polytheists be expelled from this Peninsula and that there not be left two religions herein. This is the cradle of Islam and the place of the beginning of the Message. It is not allowed for any religion except for the religion of truth, the religion of Islam, to be left in this Peninsula. May Allâh grant Muslims the ability to follow the truth and to be steadfast in it. May Allâh also guide the others to enter into Islam and leave what goes against it.

Second, it is sanctioned for you to call them to Islam and to explain to them its excellence. You may also show them what is wrong with their religion and how it opposes the truth. Also explain to them that the Law of Islam abrogates all previous laws. Tell them that Islam is the religion of truth that Allâh sent all of His Messengers with revealed the Books. Allâh has said:

﴿ إِنَّ ٱلدِّينَ عِندَ ٱللَّهِ ٱلْإِسْلَٰمُ ﴾ [آل عمران: ١٩]

"Truly, the religion with Allâh is Islam." (V. 3:19)

Allâh also says:

﴿ وَمَن يَبْتَغِ غَيْرَ ٱلْإِسْلَٰمِ دِينًا فَلَن يُقْبَلَ مِنْهُ وَهُوَ فِي ٱلْأَخِرَةِ مِنَ ٱلْخَٰسِرِينَ ﴾ [آل عمران: ٨٥]

"And whoever seeks a religion other than Islam, it will never be accepted of him and in the Hereafter he will be one of the losers." (V. 3:85)

However, you have no right to speak about that except on the basis of knowledge and understanding. Speaking about Allâh's religion without knowledge is a great evil. Allâh has stated:

﴿ قُلْ إِنَّمَا حَرَّمَ رَبِّيَ ٱلْفَوَٰحِشَ مَا ظَهَرَ مِنْهَا وَمَا بَطَنَ وَٱلْإِثْمَ وَٱلْبَغْيَ بِغَيْرِ ٱلْحَقِّ وَأَن تُشْرِكُوا۟ بِٱللَّهِ مَا لَمْ يُنَزِّلْ بِهِۦ سُلْطَٰنًا وَأَن تَقُولُوا۟ عَلَى ٱللَّهِ مَا لَا تَعْلَمُونَ ﴾ [الأعراف: ٣٣]

"Say: The things that my Lord has forbidden are illicit acts, whether committed openly or secretly, sins (of all kinds), unrighteous oppression, joining partners (in worship) with Allâh for which He has given no authority, and saying things about Allâh of which you have no knowledge." (V. 7:33)

Allâh has put the gravity of speaking about Him without knowledge above all of the acts mentioned in the Verse. This indicates how greatly forbidden it is and what a great sin it is.

Allâh also says:

﴿ قُلْ هَٰذِهِۦ سَبِيلِيٓ أَدْعُوٓا۟ إِلَى ٱللَّهِ عَلَىٰ بَصِيرَةٍ أَنَا۠ وَمَنِ ٱتَّبَعَنِي وَسُبْحَٰنَ ٱللَّهِ وَمَآ أَنَا۠ مِنَ ٱلْمُشْرِكِينَ ﴾ [يوسف: ١٠٨]

"Say: This is my way, I invite unto Allâh with sure knowledge, I and whosoever follows me (must also invite with sure knowledge). Glorified be Allâh. And I am not one of the idolaters." (V. 12:108)

49

In *Sûrat Al-Baqarah*, Allâh states that speaking about Allâh without knowledge is one of the actions that is ordered by Satan:

﴿ يَٰٓأَيُّهَا ٱلنَّاسُ كُلُوا۟ مِمَّا فِى ٱلْأَرْضِ حَلَٰلًا طَيِّبًا وَلَا تَتَّبِعُوا۟ خُطُوَٰتِ ٱلشَّيْطَٰنِ إِنَّهُۥ لَكُمْ عَدُوٌّ مُّبِينٌ ○ إِنَّمَا يَأْمُرُكُم بِٱلسُّوٓءِ وَٱلْفَحْشَآءِ وَأَن تَقُولُوا۟ عَلَى ٱللَّهِ مَا لَا تَعْلَمُونَ ﴾ [البقرة: ١٦٨، ١٦٩]

"O mankind! Eat of that which is lawful and good on the earth, and follow not the footsteps of Satan. Verily, he is to you an open enemy. (Satan) commands you only to what is evil and sinful, and that you should say against Allâh what you know not." (V. 2:168,169)

I ask Allâh for me and you support, guidance and goodness.

Sheikh Ibn Baz

Wearing *Hijâb* in the presence of the son-in-law

Q. Some women wear *Hijâb* in front of their son-in-laws and they refuse to greet them by shaking their hands. Is this allowed for them or not?

A. The son-in-law is a *Mahram* for the woman due to marriage. It is allowed for him to see of her what he can see of his mother, sister, daughter and other *Mahram* women. Covering her face, hair, forearms and so forth from her son-in-law is a type of extremism in religion. Refusing to shake his hand when meeting him is also a kind of extremism. That may lead to hard feelings and cutting off the relations between them. Therefore, she should not be extreme in this matter, unless she has some suspicion about him or she does not like the way he looks at her. In that case, what she is doing is acceptable.

The Standing Committee

50

Woman cutting hair

Q. I hope you will help me concerning cutting my hair from the front of it in a certain style wherein the hair sometimes falls down over the eyebrows of a Muslim woman. Is this allowed or not? May Allâh reward you.

A. I do not know of anything (wrong) in cutting a woman's hair. It is not allowed to shave all of it off. You cannot shave off the hair of your head but you may shorten its length. I do not know of anything wrong with that. However, that should be done in a good way that is pleasing to you and your husband. You should agree upon how it is going to be done. Also, it should not be in imitation of the disbelieving women. If you leave it long, it makes it more difficult to wash it and tend to it. If it is long or thick and a women cuts it short or layers it, there is nothing wrong with that. Or she may cut part of it short to make herself more beautiful to herself and her husband. I do not know of anything wrong with that. However, one may not shave all of it off. This is not allowed except in the case of some disease or problem.

Sheikh Ibn Baz

High-heeled shoes

Q. What is the Islamic ruling concerning wearing high-heeled shoes?

A. The least that can be said is that it is disliked. First, it is a kind of deception because it makes the woman look taller than she is. Second, it is dangerous for the woman because it is easy to fall in them. Third, it has negative health consequences as the doctors have concluded.

Sheikh Ibn Baz

No harm in the presence of a blind man

Q. Is it allowed for a woman to uncover her face in the presence of a blind man? If she cannot uncover her face, what is the legal reason preventing her to do so?

A. The correct opinion is that there is no harm in a woman uncovering her face in the presence of a blind man. A woman is ordered to cover herself in front of those who can see her in order for no temptation to arise. A blind man cannot see what is in front of him and he cannot look at what will excite him in a woman, nor is he conscious of it. There is the *Hadith* that is recorded by At-Tirmidhi, who called it *Sahih*, concerning the story of Ibn Umm Maktum, where the Prophet ﷺ (told Umm Salamah and Maimuna رضى الله عنهما) to wear *Hijâb* in front of him. (When they asked about it,) he said:

«أَفَعَمْيَاوَانِ أَنْتُمَا أَلَسْتُمَا تُبْصِرَانِهِ» .

"Are you two blind? Do you not see him?"

However, this *Hadith* is considered weak by some scholars. Even assuming it is authentic, it is concerned with the woman looking at the man. Women are also ordered to lower their gaze and it is not allowed for a woman to look at a man if her desires may be stirred, regardless of whether he be blind or seeing. In fact, she should not, in that case, even look at pictures in the newspapers or in the movies if such may occur.

Sheikh Ibn Jibreen

Uncovering hair in front of non-Muslim women

Q. Is it allowed for a Muslim woman to uncover her hair in front of non-Muslim women, especially if she describes the Muslim women to her male non-Muslim relatives?

A. This question revolves around a difference of opinion concerning the interpretation of the Verse:

﴿ وَقُل لِّلْمُؤْمِنَاتِ يَغْضُضْنَ مِنْ أَبْصَارِهِنَّ وَيَحْفَظْنَ فُرُوجَهُنَّ وَلَا يُبْدِينَ زِينَتَهُنَّ إِلَّا مَا ظَهَرَ مِنْهَا وَلْيَضْرِبْنَ بِخُمُرِهِنَّ عَلَى جُيُوبِهِنَّ وَلَا يُبْدِينَ زِينَتَهُنَّ إِلَّا لِبُعُولَتِهِنَّ أَوْ ءَابَآئِهِنَّ أَوْ ءَابَآءِ بُعُولَتِهِنَّ أَوْ أَبْنَآئِهِنَّ أَوْ أَبْنَآءِ بُعُولَتِهِنَّ أَوْ إِخْوَٰنِهِنَّ أَوْ بَنِىٓ إِخْوَٰنِهِنَّ أَوْ بَنِىٓ أَخَوَٰتِهِنَّ أَوْ نِسَآئِهِنَّ أَوْ مَا مَلَكَتْ أَيْمَٰنُهُنَّ أَوِ ٱلتَّٰبِعِينَ غَيْرِ أُوْلِى ٱلْإِرْبَةِ مِنَ ٱلرِّجَالِ أَوِ ٱلطِّفْلِ ٱلَّذِينَ لَمْ يَظْهَرُوا عَلَىٰ عَوْرَٰتِ ٱلنِّسَآءِ ﴾

[النور : ٣١]

"Tell the believing women to lower their gaze and protect their private parts and not to show off their adornments except that which is apparent and to draw their veils over necks and bosoms and not to reveal their adornments except to their husbands, their fathers, their husband's fathers, their sons, their husband's sons, their brothers or their brother's sons, or their sister's sons, or their women or the (female) slaves, or old male servants who lack vigor, or small children who have no sense of the shame of sex." (V. 24:31)

There is a difference of opinion concerning the referent of the pronoun in the phrase: "their women." Some say that it refers to the class of women as a whole. Some say that it refers to the described women only, that is, the believing women. According to the first opinion, a woman may uncover her face and hands in front of a non-Muslim woman. According to the second opinion, a Muslim woman may not do so. I am more inclined to the first opinion and believe it is more likely to be correct. That is because when a woman is in the presence of another woman, it makes no difference if that woman is a Muslim or not, as long as there is no kind of temptation involved. However, if one fears something of that nature, such as the woman describing the Muslim women to

53

her male relatives, then one must avoid such a case and then the woman should not uncover her face or any part of her body in front of such a woman. This is true regardless of whether that troublesome woman is a Muslim or a non-Muslim.

Sheikh Ibn Uthaimin

Wearing light colored and short dresses

Q. What is the ruling concerning wearing light colored clothing, such as yellow, white or red, but which covers the body? What is the ruling concerning wearing short clothing that expose the legs?

A. It is allowed for a woman to wear whatever clothing is normal for the women to wear, as long as it is not something to be specifically recognized as that for men. In that case, a woman should not wear it as the Prophet ﷺ cursed the women who imitate men and vice versa.

Woman must wear clothing that covers her entire body if she is in the presence of men she is not related to. She may not uncover anything of her body to them, not her face, hands or feet except in cases of need, such as handing or taking something and so forth. She also cannot wear tight clothing that shows her body shape or the size of parts of her body, such as her breasts, shoulders, chest, buttocks and so forth. One must also bring up one's children accustomed to wearing long, flowing garments. If a child grows up accustomed to something, it is very difficult to get them away from it when they get older. If the dress is short, it may show the attractiveness of her body and shows to men what will be a temptation or cause of temptation for them. There is no harm if a woman, in her house and in the presence of her relatives, wears a short dress due to some need, even if it shows her shins or upper arm, as women usually wear when they have to work.

Sheikh Ibn Jibreen

Wearing gloves

Q. Is wearing socks or gloves on the hands in order to cover them an innovation or is it permissible? Is it forbidden for a non-*Mahram* male to see a woman's hand if there is no adornment on it? Is it permissible for one spouse to prevent the other from fulfilling his or her natural right (to sexual intercourse) for a lengthy period of time without any acceptable *Shari'ah* excuse?

A It is obligatory upon a woman to wear whatever covers her body and private parts, especially if she is going out to the market or someplace similar. Therefore, she may wear socks over her feet and gloves over her hands so that nothing that could be a temptation may be seen of her. However, exposing the hand without a glove on it is permissible if there is some need, as long as the hand is not adorned with dye, jewelry or anything of that nature. This is the case since hands almost all look alike among the people.

There is no doubt that there is a psychological need for sexual contact between the two spouses. Usually, the wants of the two differ, based on different levels of desire between the man and the woman. Usually the man's desire is stronger. Therefore, he is usually the one desiring the act more. In fact, many wives complain about their husbands and the extent to which they desire sexual contact, to the point that it harms the woman.

As for avoiding such contact for a long time, this is not allowed. The woman has a right to have her needs fulfilled. The most that a woman can be asked to be patient for is four months. Therefore, the desires and needs of both should be met. The desires, abilities and shortcomings of both parties should be taken into consideration without either party being harmed.

Sheikh Ibn Jibreen

Shaking hands with women

Q. What is the ruling on exchanging handshake with women?

A. It is not permissible for a man to exchange a handshake with women who are not his *Mahram*. Upon receiving the pledge of obedience from women, the Prophet ﷺ said to them: "I do not shake hands with women." 'Âishah, the wife of the Prophet ﷺ asserted: "By Allâh, the hand of the Messenger of Allâh ﷺ never touched a hand of a woman. He only accepted their pledges verbally." Allâh the Exalted says: "Verily, you have in the Messenger of Allâh an excellent model, for him who fears Allâh and the Last Day, and who remembers Allâh much."

There is no harm, however, in exchanging verbal greeting with women which is void of tempting soft speech. Allâh says: "O wives of the Prophet! You are not like any other women if you are righteous. So be not soft in speech, lest he in whose heart is a disease should feel tempted; and speak to men in a decent manner."

There is no harm for women to shake the hands of their fathers, brothers, uncles, or any other *Mahram* of theirs.

Sheikh Ibn Baz

Ridiculing woman's dress code

Q. What is the ruling on the case of a person who derides the *Hijâb*, and makes fun of Muslim women who cover their faces and hands in public?

A. A person who makes fun of a *Muslimah* who observes the Islamic dress code becomes a *Kâfir* or an apostate. Abdullâh bin 'Umar رضى الله عنــهما reported: During the mission of Tabûk, a man said: "We have never seen like our scholars; they have the largest stomachs, and lie the most, and are the most cowardly in the battlefield." A man responded to him angrily and said: "You are a liar. You are a hypocrite. I shall certainly report you to the Messenger of Allâh ﷺ." The Messenger of Allâh ﷺ was informed about the incident. He received Qur'ânic revelation concerning the abusive statement. Abdullâh bin 'Umar said: I have seen the man who made the statement hanging on to the reign of the she-camel of the Messenger of Allâh ﷺ with his feet bleeding being dragged on stones pleading with the Prophet ﷺ: "O Rasulullâh! We were only amusing ourselves by vain talk." The Messenger of Allâh ﷺ was only reciting the Qur'ânic words that were revealed spontaneously: "Say was it Allâh and His *Âyât* (signs) and His Messenger that you mocked at? Offer no excuse. You have certainly apostatized after believing." With these words Allâh the Exalted has equated deriding the believers as deriding , His *Âyât*, and His Messenger ﷺ.

The Standing Committee

A wig for beauty

Q. Is it lawful for a woman to wear a wig or a hairpiece in order to beautify herself for her husband?

A. It is the duty of both spouses to beautify themselves for each other, but within the limits of the *Shari'ah* avoiding the unlawful means of beautification. Wearing wigs is a fad that was common among the disbelievers to the point that it has become prototypical of theirs. Therefore, wearing wigs by a Muslim woman even for beautifying herself for her husband signifies resembling the disbelievers. The Prophet ﷺ prohibited imitating the disbelievers saying: "He who imitates certain people, he would be considered as one of them." The prohibition which applies to wearing a wig applies to wearing a hairpiece, even harsher. The Prophet ﷺ forbade wearing it and cursed both those who wear them and those who manufacture them.

The Standing Committee

Plucking eyebrows and growing fingernails

Q. What is the ruling on the case of plucking eyebrows, growing fingernails, and applying nail polish on them?

A. It is not permissible to take all or part of the eyebrows. It is authentically reported that the Prophet 醬 cursed the one who plucks her own eyebrows and the one who plucks others.

Growing fingernails is against the *Sunnah*. It is authentically reported that the Prophet 醬 said: "Five things are from the *Fitrah*:[6] circumcision, shaving off the pubic hair, trimming mustaches, plucking, or shaving off armpit hair and clipping the fingernails and toenails." The Prophet 醬 instructed that they should not be left undone for a period longer than forty days. Neglecting them would make man resemble animals and some of the disbelievers.

As for nail polish, it is better not to apply it. If it is applied, it should be removed prior to performing *Wudu'* for it prevents water from reaching the surface of the fingernails.

Sheikh Ibn Baz

The Muslim women of that land must not obey Its rulers

Q. A law was passed by the rulers of a Muslim land forcing the young women and all women to remove their *Hijâb*, in particular their face coverings. Is it permissible for me to

---

[6] The *Fitrah,* the conduct pursued and prescribed, to be followed by Allâh's Messenger 醬.

execute that order? You should also realize that the one who refuses to obey that command will be punished by, for example, removal from work or school or imprisonment.

A.   This trial that has befallen your land is from those events by which the slaves are tested and tried. Allâh has said in the Qur'ân:

﴿ أَحَسِبَ ٱلنَّاسُ أَن يُتْرَكُوٓا أَن يَقُولُوٓا ءَامَنَّا وَهُمْ لَا يُفْتَنُونَ ۝ وَلَقَدْ فَتَنَّا ٱلَّذِينَ مِن قَبْلِهِمْ فَلَيَعْلَمَنَّ ٱللَّهُ ٱلَّذِينَ صَدَقُوا وَلَيَعْلَمَنَّ ٱلْكَٰذِبِينَ ﴾

[العنكبوت: ٢، ٣]

"Do people think that they will be left alone because they say, 'We believe,' and will not be tested. And We indeed tested those who were before them. And Allâh will certainly make (it) known (the truth of) those who are true, and will certainly make (it) known (the falsehood of) those who are liars." (V. 29:2-3)

In my opinion, it is obligatory upon the Muslim sisters of that land to refuse to obey the rulers in that evil order. This is because there is no obedience to evil and rejected orders. Allâh says:

﴿ يَٰٓأَيُّهَا ٱلَّذِينَ ءَامَنُوٓا أَطِيعُوا ٱللَّهَ وَأَطِيعُوا ٱلرَّسُولَ وَأُوْلِي ٱلْأَمْرِ مِنكُمْ ﴾

[النساء: ٥٩]

"O you who believe! Obey Allâh and obey the Messenger and those of you who are in authority." (V. 4:59)

If one ponders over this Verse, one notes that Allâh has stated: "Obey Allâh and obey the Messenger and those of you who are in authority." That is, the word "obey" is not repeated directly before "those of you who are in authority." This indicates that obedience to those in authority is conditional upon obedience to Allâh and obedience to His Messenger. If their orders are in contradiction to obedience to Allâh and His Messenger, then they are not to be listened to or obeyed in that matter that they have ordered.

59

«لَا طَاعَةَ لِمَخْلُوقٍ فِي مَعْصِيةِ الْخَالِقِ»

"There is no obedience to the created if it involves disobedience to the Creator."[7]

The hurt that these women face in this matter is part of what one must be patient with. They must seek 's help in being patient. We ask Allâh to guide their leaders to the truth.

I do not think that such a compulsion can exist unless the woman leaves her house. In her house, it is not possible that they could force such a thing upon her. Hence, the sisters should try to stay in their houses until the matter is rectified. If her studies involve a disobedience to Allâh, then her studies are not permissible. Instead, she should study what she needs for her religion and worldly needs and, usually, this can be done in her household. In sum, it is never allowed to obey the rulers in a command that is an evil and wrong in itself.

Sheikh Ibn Uthaimin

Wearing tight clothing and white clothing

Q. Is it allowed for a woman to wear tight clothing? Is it allowed for her to wear white clothing?

A. It is not allowed for women to be in front of non-related men or in public streets or marketplaces while she is wearing tight clothing that describes her body to anyone who looks at her. This makes it like she is naked and stirring temptations. It is a cause for great evil. She also may not wear white clothing because in our country the white clothing is something specific and recognizable for men. In that case, she would be resembling men and the Prophet ﷺ cursed those women who resembled men.

The Standing Committee

---

[7] With this wording, this is a *Hadith* recorded by *Ahmad*. However, *Muslim* has something very close to it.

Being held accountable for what one wears

Q. Is it correct that a person will be held accountable on the Day of Resurrection for what clothing he wore?

A. Yes, the person will be asked about his wealth and where he acquired it from and what he spent on it. This is stated in a *Hadith*.

Shaikh Ibn Baz

There is no harm in joking as long as it is truthful

Q. What is the ruling concerning joking? Is it considered useless and vain speech? Note that it does not contain any ridiculing of the religion.

A. There is no harm in joking by words and anecdotes, if they are truthful and real, especially if it is not done often. The Prophet ﷺ used to jest but he would only speak the truth. If it is with lying, then it is not allowed. The Prophet ﷺ said:

"Woe to the one who speaks and tells a lie in order to make the people laugh at it. Woe to him. Then again, woe to him."

This was recorded by Abu Dawud, At-Tirmidhi and An-Nasa'i with a good chain.

Shaikh Ibn Baz

Wash or wipe over the hair?

Q. Is it compulsory to wash your hair during an obligatory bath or can women just wet their hair or wipe over them with a wet hand?

A. If taking an obligatory bath, it is compulsory for both men and women to wet their whole body. If any part remains dry, that bath is not acceptable, making one unable to pray. Regarding the hair, the Prophet ﷺ has emphasised to completely wet the roots of the hair. If any woman has long hair and faces difficulty washing all her hair, then she should at least wet the hair to the roots. (There is no need to wipe over the remaining hair as long as the roots are wet.)

Maulana Mahmood Ahmad Mirpuri

Treatment by a male doctor

Q. If we don't have access to female doctors, can our wives and daughters be treated by a male doctor? Some people consider it very wrong.

A. If there are no facilities of a female doctor, then there is no harm in being treated by a male doctor. Those who think it is totally wrong, may do so by tradition, but this is not an Islamic opinion. Islam does not give permission to put one's life in danger, and some illnesses require immediate attention, therefore there is no harm in visiting a male doctor.

Maulana Mahmood Ahmad Mirpuri

Circular shaped gold jewelry

Q. What is the ruling concerning circular shaped gold jewelry?[8]

A. It is permissible for women to wear either circular shaped or non-circular shaped gold jewelry. This is based on the general meaning of the Verse:

﴿ أَوَمَن يُنَشَّؤُا۟ فِى ٱلْحِلْيَةِ وَهُوَ فِى ٱلْخِصَامِ غَيْرُ مُبِينٍ ﴾

[الزخرف : ١٨]

---

[8] This question may sound strange at first glance. However, the obvious reason behind it is that some scholars are of the opinion that such jewelry is not allowed for women although women may wear gold jewelry of other shapes.

"(Do they then like for Allâh) a creature who is brought up in adornments and in dispute cannot make herself clear?" (V. 43:18)

Allah has mentioned that wearing jewelry is a characteristic of women. This is general and covers gold as well as other jewelry. Furthermore, Ahmad, Abu Dawud and An-Nasa'i record with a good chain from 'Ali bin Abu Tâlib that the Prophet ﷺ took silk in his right hand and gold in his left and then said:

"These two are forbidden for the males of my nation."

In the narration by Ibn Mâjah, it ends,

"And permissible for its women."

Also, Ahmad, An-Nasa'i, At-Tirmidhi— who said it is *Sahih*— Abu Dâwud, Al-Hâkim— who also called it *Sahih*— At-Tabarâni and Ibn Hazm— who again said it is *Sahih*— all record from Abu Musa Al-Ash'ari that the Prophet ﷺ said:

"Gold and silk have been made permissible for the females of my nation and forbidden for its males."

Shaikh Ibn Baz

Does a woman act as a *Mahram* for another woman

Q. Can a woman be considered a *Mahram* for a woman she is not related to for purposes of traveling or sitting with others?

A. A woman cannot be a *Mahram* for another. The one who is considered *Mahram* is a man that a woman cannot marry due to blood relations, such as her father and her brother, or a man related to her due to marriage, such as her husband, her father-in-law and her step-son, or a man related due to breastfeeding, such as her father from breastfeeding and so forth.

It is not allowed for a man to be in private with a woman he is not related to, nor can he travel with her. The Prophet ﷺ said:

«لَا تُسَافِرِ امْرَأَةٌ إِلَّا مَعَ ذِي مَحْرِمٍ»

"A woman does not travel except with a *Mahram*."

This was recorded by Al-Bukhâri and Muslim. The Prophet ﷺ also said:

«لَا يَخْلُوَنَّ رَجُلٌ بِامْرَأَةٍ فَإِنَّ الشَّيْطَانَ ثَالِثُهُمَا».

"A man is never alone with a woman except that Satan is the third."

This was recorded by Imam Ahmad and others from the *Hadith* of 'Umar رضى الله عنه with a *Sahih* chain.

Shaikh Ibn Baz